Almost There

A 28 day devotional journey for
High School Seniors

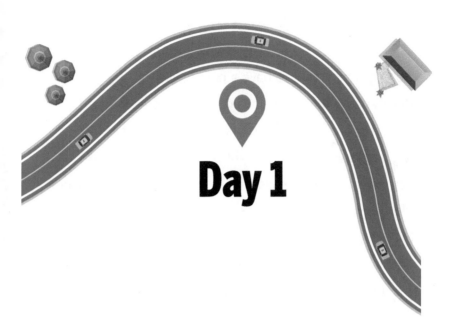

Day 1

With all the change senior year can bring, you may find yourself hitting some low points where you feel like you lack direction on what to do or where to go. On those days, be sure to seek wise counsel. The hard days can sometimes overwhelm us, making us feel stuck, so getting wise counsel from outside of your circle – from someone who is further along than you in life, who can encourage you where you are in this current stage, is important. Call it a mentor, a counselor, an advisor—whatever you want.

Just find someone older and wiser who is willing to invest in you and love you, someone who you can be real and vulnerable with and who can hold you accountable. It may not seem like a big deal now, but at some point this year, you're going to want to have a person like this in your life. And it's better to have an idea of who that person might be now, before you feel like you need it. Because the truth is, as great as your parents might be, there are some things they won't be able to speak into. Having someone who can listen to you, who you can trust, who won't shame you or think of you differently is a game changer. Navigating life requires making tough decisions and seeking wise counsel to pour into those decisions as we walk through both the mountains and the valleys will make the difficult moments easier. Proverbs 24:6, communicates this very idea by saying,

"For by wise guidance you can wage your war, and in an abundance of counselors there is victory."

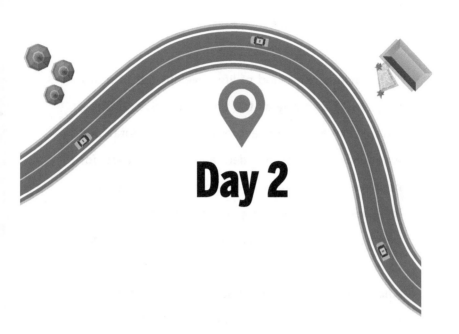

Day 2

You should know that following Jesus isn't always considered "popular." Making good or wise decisions can be frowned upon by those who aren't making the same kind of decisions for themselves. You may find yourself being judged or looked down on for how you decide to live your life, but believe me, following Jesus is worth it. Long term, you will not regret choosing his way. Chances are, you will not look back on your senior year or any other stage of life and think, "Wow I really wish I wouldn't have made that good decision" or "I regret being wise in that situation." God's way leaves you with less regret. The apostle Paul writes about it this way in Galatians 5:19-21,

"It is obvious what kind of life develops out of trying to get your own way all the time: repetitive, loveless, cheap sex; a stinking accumulation of mental and emotional garbage; frenzied and joyless grabs for happiness; trinket gods; magic-show religion; paranoid loneliness; cutthroat competition; all-consuming-yet-never-satisfied wants; a brutal temper; an impotence to love or be loved; divided homes and divided lives; small-minded and lopsided pursuits; the vicious habit of depersonalizing everyone into a rival; uncontrolled and uncontrollable addictions; ugly parodies of community. I could go on. This isn't the first time I have warned you, you know. If you use your freedom this way, you will not inherit God's kingdom" (MSG).

In other words, we can't always trust ourselves to go after the right thing. But when we use our freedom to go after God's way, it ultimately leads to the life God wants for us.

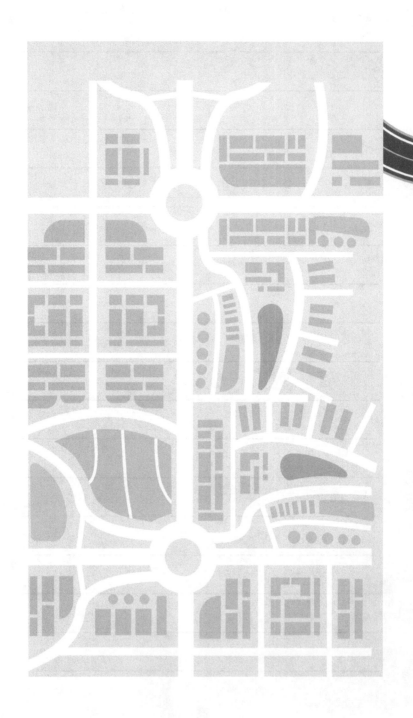

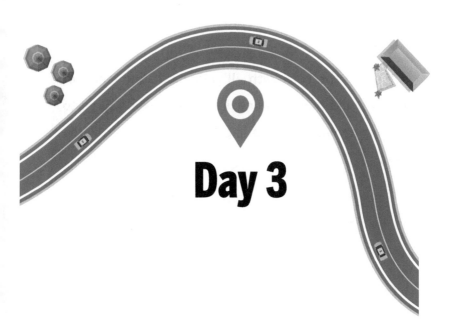

Day 3

Maybe you've already discovered this to be true, but life is a rollercoaster. Specifically, high school can be a rollercoaster—especially your senior year being full of both firsts and lasts. One day you can experience the highest of highs and the next, the lowest of lows. Sometimes you can experience both in a matter of minutes! But no matter where you may be in the roller coaster today or tomorrow, the best thing to remember in both the highs and the lows is that God will see you through. The Lord will always lift you back up the hill you face. He will never ever leave your side. Do not give up trusting in him and his plan. A verse from the book of Proverbs says it this way:

"Trust in the Lord with all your heart and lean not on your own understanding; in all your ways submit to him and he will make your paths straight."(Proverbs 3:5-6.)

No matter what the current roller coaster looks like, God is worth trusting.

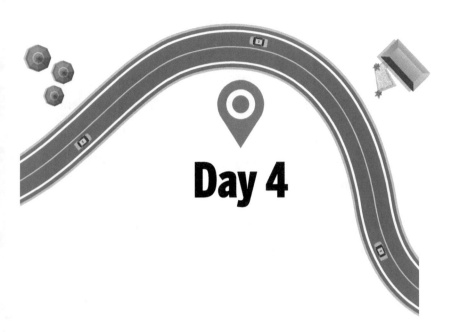

Day 4

You won't always agree with your parents. This probably isn't a surprise to you. And the good news is, it's okay to not always agree with them. Especially as you move towards more independence, you are going to discover more and more that you are your own person, with your own thoughts and opinions. That's a good thing. But just because you may not agree with your parents on everything, doesn't mean you're always going to be right and they're always going to be wrong. In fact, I've learned, in some way or another, parents are right more often than I think. Try to keep that in mind the next time you find yourself in an argument with them. Even more than that—this last year before a season of a lot of change—do everything you can to love them, and respect them in the time you have with them. Because as much as they may annoy you at times, the truth is, they are one or two of the few people who will be a constant throughout your life. Not only that, God cares about how you treat your parents. The fifth of the famous Ten Commandments tells us:

"Honor your father and your mother, so that you may live long in the land the LORD your God is giving you. – Exodus 20:12

We don't have to agree with them. But we must honor them. As you go through your senior year, do everything you can to walk through conversations with them showing respect. Take advantage of your time with them, and do your best to try and see where they are coming from . Give them the honor and credit they deserve. Maybe that honor looks like forgiving your parent(s) for something you felt they did wrong. As difficult as it may be, forgiving them is good for you. Whether it's for something big or something small, work on forgiving your parents as a way of honoring them and respecting them. Look for ways to practice honor this year before your relationship with them changes next year. And remember, your parents are human too, just doing the best they can, so give them grace.

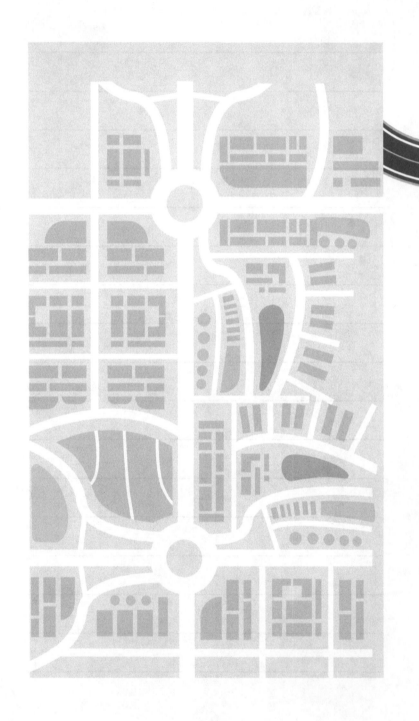

Day 5

Have you ever noticed there's a place in your house where loose change starts to pile up? Maybe it's the center console of your car, or a jar on your desk, or maybe for you super organized people, you just keep it in your wallet. The thing about loose change is, most of us don't really even treat it like it's money, unless the change is in bulk. A dime on the ground may not get our attention, but a jar full of dimes? That's a month's worth of laundry money next year! The more there is, the more we seem to care. This is true in life as well. Every day we experience change, whether that's changes in schedules, class periods, due dates for school assignments, appointments or meetings. And for the most part these changes don't get much of our attention. But when it comes to big change, it's different. This last year of high school is the start of some big change—change in life chapters, friends, schools, or jobs. This kind of change gets a lot of our mental energy. These big changes cause us to stress and worry more than usual, creating anxious thoughts of the "what ifs" that may result from that change. The uncertainty of what's next can dominate our thinking, and not always in a positive way. But what if we started to see change as not something to fear, but an opportunity for growth? Often, change can be a really great thing, and all it takes is for us to change our perspective. Philippians 4:6-8 says:

> **"Do not be anxious about anything, but in every situation, by prayer and petition, with thanksgiving, present your requests to God. And the peace of God, which transcends all understanding, will guard your hearts and your minds in Christ Jesus. Finally, brothers and sisters, whatever is true, whatever is noble, whatever is right, whatever is pure, whatever is lovely, whatever is admirable- if anything is excellent or praiseworthy- think about such things."**

Heading into a year with more big changes ahead, these words from Philippians will be good to keep in mind.

Day 6

Over the course of my senior year there were three lessons that I learned over and over again. 1) Patience is so powerful, 2) Quality matters more than quantity, and 3) Being present in all you do is important. Over the next few weeks we'll look at all three of these, but this week we'll start with the power of patience.

No one enjoys learning patience. Everyone from toddlers to adults struggle with it. Whether it's trying to be patient in line at an amusement park, or being patient while you wait for the pizza to be delivered, it's never easy. Not being able to have what we want is frustrating and discouraging. Which is why it can be helpful to remember that even when we are impatient waiting for what we want, God knows how it will all unfold. Romans 8:25 says,

"But if we hope for what we do not have, we wait for it patiently."

Later, in the book of Galatians, the apostle Paul describes patience as a fruit of the spirit, meaning it's something that reflects God's spirit at work in us. Every day is an opportunity to learn to become more like God as we wait for the things we want. And as hard as it can be to learn to develop this quality, it's something we will never regret having learned to be. Our life pictures are not ours to paint so let the Lord take hold of the brush.

Day 7

Quality matters more than Quantity. If I was asked what ONE thing God taught me the most about in my Senior year it would be this idea. Quality matters more than quantity. There were a lot of years, where I cared far more about being popular and having a large number of friends more than I did about the quality of friends I had. I worried over how big my "crew" was and how many people around the school "knew my name". It took longer than I'd like to admit for me to realize how CRAZY, SILLY, and UNFAIR this was to myself and how it was hurting my relationship with God. I had to learn good friends come in quality not quantity.

I was wanting popularity for all the wrong reasons—as a way to find value and worth. Quality friends are the kind who will lead you in faith, challenge you with questions, and support you when things are difficult. These are the friendships we need to fight to have. Not necessarily a high number of friends but the kind of friends you can count on to help shape you into the best version of yourself. These are the friends you want to invest in. Like Proverbs 18:24 says,

"A man of many companions may come to ruin, but there is a friend that sticks closer than a brother."

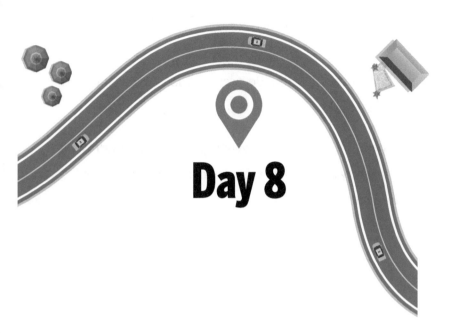

Day 8

Being present in all you do is important. The idea of learning how to be present was something it took me a lot of my senior year to learn how to do. You've probably been told this idea so many times: be present in the moment, don't get stuck in the past, don't look too far ahead in the future. But there may be no other time when learning to be present matters more than your senior year. It's your last year in school, your last summer at home in this stage, and it is so important to not wish this time away for what's next. Work hard at being purposeful with your presence this year. Because it turns out what everyone says is true: this year WILL fly by, and you'll regret it if you wish it away. Whether you are excited about what comes next or dreading it, do the best you can to stay present mentally and emotionally these next few months. Be present today and remember what Jesus said in Matthew 6:34,

> "Therefore do not worry about tomorrow, for tomorrow will worry about itself. Each day has enough trouble of its own."

Day 9

In Matthew 18:3, Jesus says we must:

"turn and become like children, [or else] you will never enter the kingdom of heaven."

Have you ever hung around little kids before? If they aren't your own younger brother or sister driving you crazy, it doesn't take long to realize that kids just have this ability to be all in the moment. You don't have to teach a child joy. You don't have to teach a child happiness. You don't have to teach a child to soak up the moment they are in. Not only that, they have a level of trust and confidence in the adults who take care of them. There's something about how easily a child trusts and expresses what they are feeling that makes me think this is what Jesus had in mind when he tells us to become like them. Imagine what it would be like to trust that easily in Jesus and his care for us? Imagine what it would be like to be able to express what you are feeling without fear of being judged or looked down on or misunderstood? If we are to become like children, than that means we have to come to a place of trust and confidence in the God who promises to take care of us, trusting him with everything from our fears to our future. We can trust Jesus like a little kid trusts the world around them. We don't have to be afraid that Jesus can't handle what we throw at him.

_____

_____

_____

_____

_____

_____

_____

_____

_____

_____

_____

_____

_____

_____

_____

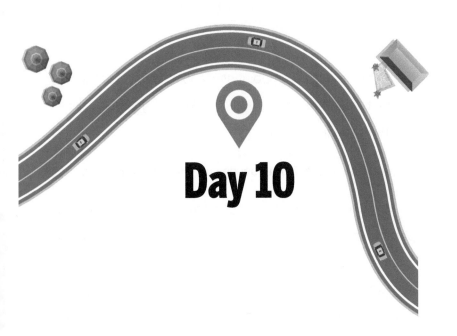

Day 10

You may find this last year of high school is a time where you are learning more and more about how you are wired and what makes you, you. This is a super helpful time to learn this about yourself, because next year, where there is so much change, having a self-awareness about yourself will better prepare you for the change. For me, I learned that I was very indecisive, and also a total people person. I love the company, advice, and companionship of people. And there is nothing wrong with that, except sometimes I tend to rely a little too much on people in decisions where I should be trusting God. I still ask the Lord to help me in my indecisiveness and overreliance on others. Not long ago I realized that a lot of my indecisiveness and relying on other people was coming from fear. Fear of making the wrong decisions, fear of disappointing people, fear I didn't have what it takes to move forward. In Luke 5:10, Jesus is talking to Simon and Jesus tells him:

"Don't be afraid; from now on you will fish for people."

That phrase, "don't be afraid" is one of the most repeated phrases in all of Scripture. And for me, hearing from Jesus that I shouldn't be afraid was a big deal. It's easy to fall back into worry and anxious thoughts, but when we begin to pray truths over ourselves, the fear begins to disappear. Where the Lord is, fear loses power. Where the Lord is, worry loses power. Where the Lord is, anxiety loses power. Where the Lord is, there is strength. Where the Lord is, there is comfort. Where the Lord is, there is peace. Pray that you will not allow fear to fill you, that you will be learn to "fear not" because of God's presence in your life.

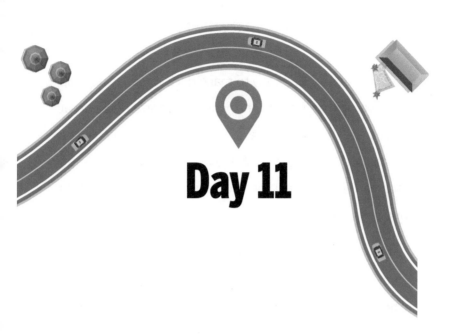

Day 11

All of us have an idea of what our future will look like. We imagine our future when it comes to relationships, academics, careers, and friendships. Even more amazing, God has a plan for our future as well, and it's a plan we get to participate in. The biggest factor in following the Lord's path for us is our own decisions. Bad decisions cost us, and good ones benefit us. That doesn't mean God will give up on you if you make a bad decision. He will never give up on you. He reaches out to you with his arms wide open, full of grace. But bad decisions cost us and effect the future we have in mind for ourselves. So how do we begin to make decisions that set us up for the future we want? We go after wisdom. We keep in mind our past, present, and future in each decision we make. When we keep in mind the future we want we are more likely to make decisions that will help us arrive at that future. And when we don't make great choices, God's grace bridges our mistakes for us. Hiding our past or ignoring it won't make it go away. But God's grace can help us deal with our past and learn from it. In Ephesians 5:15-16 it says,

> **"Be very careful, then, how you live—not as unwise, but as wise, making the most of every opportunity, because the days are evil. Therefore do not be foolish, but understand what the Lord's will is."**

The Message translation breaks these verses down into three parts:

1. Watch your step. Meaning we must keep our eyes on our OWN walk, not on those around us. Our walk is our own, not anyone else's.

2. Use your head. Oftentimes we know what the wise decision is, we just don't always have the follow through to actually do it. So we need to go after the wise thing to do, and then have the courage to actually do it.

3. Make the most out of every situation. Be present. Embrace the STEP you're in today, not tomorrow. we shouldn't get so caught up in the future and what's far up ahead that we lose focus on the present.

These are good things to do whether you are a follower of Jesus or not. So focus on your STEP, be wise in your decisions, and be present and live each day to the fullest, taking advantage of your stage of life.

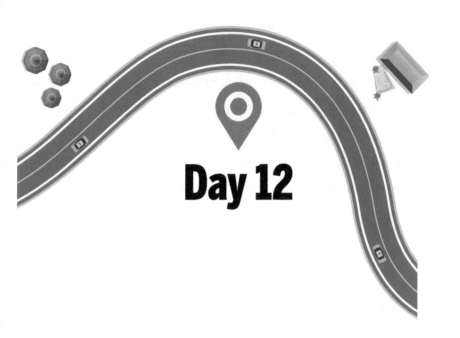

Day 12

Chances are you have experienced some difficult things in your life, or seen them happen in the world around you. Often when hard things happen we find ourselves asking, "Why?" Why did this happen? Why did that happen? Why me? Why him? Why her? Why all that hurt? Why cancer? Why sickness? Why death? Why pain? Why suffering? These are normal questions and they can sometimes leave us wondering where God is when hard things happen. Even when hard things cause us to question if God is trustworthy as a result, there are certain picture from Scripture that tell us what God is like, even when life is hard. In Luke chapter 15, Jesus shares three parables painting pictures of the love and compassion he has on all of us.

"There will be more rejoicing in heaven," (Luke 15:7) "There is rejoicing in the presence of angels of God" (Luke 15:10) "His father saw him and was filled with compassion for him" (Luke 15:20) and "For this son of mine was dead and is alive again; he was lost and is found. So they began to celebrate." (Luke 15:24).

When life gives us circumstances that cause us to wonder what God is like, verses like these from Luke remind us of what God is like. He rejoices over us. He has compassion on us. He looks out for us. He celebrates us. God isn't out to get us and he hasn't abandoned us when things are hard. We can count on what God is like when things are good and when things are bad. Even when life doesn't make sense, who God is, stays the same. And Luke isn't the only place where we get insight into what God is like. We also know God is: love (1 John 4:16), all powerful (Jeremiah 32:17), all knowing (Matthew 10:30), ever present (Psalm 139:1), mighty to save (Zephaniah 3:17), the way, the truth, and the life (John 14:6), for us (Romans 8:31).

Because we are: loved by him (John 3:16), forgiven (Colossians 1:14), redeemed from the hands of the enemy

(Psalm 107:2), NOT of this world (John 17:16) and sons and daughters of a king (Galatians 3:26). When we better know what God is like and who we are, we are better able to handle whatever life may throw at us.

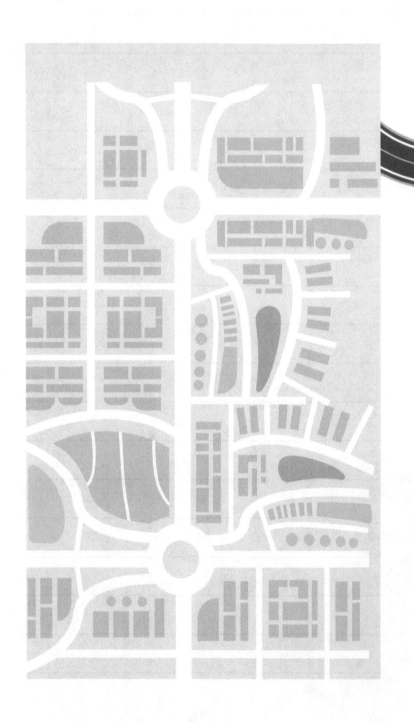

Day 13

As you go through your senior year of high school, it can feel like this season is full of endings. It's the "last" and "final" everything. But even with the end of a lot of things, don't forget there are a lot of things just starting out. Blank, new pages of your life are beginning, even as some are ending. You are almost done with high school, but you are beginning a new season of college, or work, or life on your own. You may be wrapping up a small group or losing your part of a familiar community, but you're also opening a new chapter of community. You may be done living at home with a day to day schedule, but you are about to embark on a whole new adventure with your faith. With the end of any one thing, comes the beginning of something else. Endings can be hard, and it can be tempting to stay stuck in what is coming to an end and get caught up in how sad it is. But endings can also give us an opportunity to lean into the newness of life.

Not only that, but endings give us a chance to reflect on and share what the Lord has done in and through our hearts. The end of my time in high school allowed me to see how gracious and constant God is. He moved through me and was with me in my lows and left me smiling big in my highs. As this season begins to come to an end, allow yourself to slow down, cherish the stage you are in and take the time to reflect back on what God has done in you and through you in this time.

Isaiah 43:19 says, **"See I am doing new things! Now it springs up; do you not perceive it? I am making a way in the wilderness and streams in the wasteland."**

The Message translation says it this way: "Be alert, be present. I'm about to do something brand new. It's bursting out! Don't you see it? There it is! I am making a road through the desert, rivers in the badlands."

The end of an era means new beginnings. Let this stage of life be both the ending of one thing, and the beginning of another. Reflect on your past, and know God is shaping your story one step at a time.

_____

_____

_____

_____

_____

_____

_____

_____

_____

_____

_____

_____

_____

_____

_____

_____

_____

_____

_____

_____

_____

_____

Day 14

Think about your best friend. What do you love about them? Why are you so close? I bet one of the things you love about them is that you could call them at any hour and they would be there for you. No matter what you are going through or what the circumstances are you know they will have your back. They won't let you slip, and if you get close they will be there to catch you. That's what good friends do. What would you think if we told you that God has your back in the same way?

He will not let your foot slip—

he who watches over you will not slumber;

indeed, he who watches over Israel

will neither slumber nor sleep.

The Lord watches over you—

the Lord is your shade at your right hand;

the sun will not harm you by day,

nor the moon by night.

The Lord will keep you from all harm—

he will watch over your life;

the Lord will watch over your coming and going

both now and forevermore.

- Pslam 121: 3-8

Even when you don't feel like it God is with you. He has plans for you. He is on your side.

ALMOST THERE:
A 28 DAY DEVOTIONAL JOURNEY FOR HIGH SCHOOL SENIORS

Day 15

Have you ever heard people describe this idea of a cup inside of us that gets filled up and emptied out? We empty our cup when we love someone who needs loving, or we give advice or wisdom to someone seeking counsel, or being purposeful in kindness, generosity or service towards someone who may be tough to love. In the same way our cups gets filled back up when we are loved when we need loving, or when someone gives us advice or wisdom when we need it, or when someone is kind generous and serves us in some way. The thing about this idea of a cup is that we operate best when there's an equal distribution of what's coming in and going out. In order to feel rested and full enough to pour into someone else, we need to have wisdom and love being given to us. If we don't, we feel burnt out or exhausted. I know, because I've been there. I've poured out more than I had to give and it hurt me and the people closest to me. Think of it like a literal cup of water. If you pour all the water in the cup down the drain, when you get thirsty there will be nothing left to drink. In the same way, if you pour out all of the love you have in your cup into other people's cups, when you need love yourself, you won't have anything to draw from. So how do you make sure you have what you need in your cup? I've learned God is the source of filling us back up. And he can do it through people, community, Scripture, wise counsel, time alone, being quiet or spending time outside. Figuring out what you need to refill your cup will be so helpful for you to know, and then learning how to do those things will benefit you long term. In John 6:35 Jesus says,

"I am the bread of life, whoever comes to me shall not hunger, and whoever believes in me shall not thirst."

When our cups are empty Jesus fills us back up. So surround yourself with community who loves you the way Jesus loves you. Take time to invest in his word. Seek wisdom from the wise when you are needing reassurance and encouragement. Don't let your cup get too low before taking the time to fill back up. Receive it as often as you give it. As you love and encourage others, let others love and encourage you.

_____

_____

_____

_____

_____

_____

_____

_____

_____

_____

_____

_____

_____

_____

_____

_____

_____

_____

_____

Day 16

Some things are just easier to talk about than others. And depending on how we are wired some things that may be easy for some people to talk about, may be a lot harder for others. When it comes to talking about emotions and vocalizing what we are feeling, it can be really difficult. We can find ourselves feeling a certain way but may not be sure why that's the case. We can be very easily agitated and constantly on edge. Maybe we get super emotional and everything seems to make us upset, no matter how small. Maybe the people around us notice it, or maybe we get really good at hiding how we are feeling. But not matter how it displays itself, the truth is, we have to learn how to take our emotional temperature and learn how to put words around what we are feeling. For a long time I thought I had to constantly be happy for people and made a habit out of tucking my emotions away. I didn't realize how unhealthy this was for me.

About that same time I heard a message at church that talked about the importance of grief. The speaker said it is often our habit to bury what we are feeling and replace the unhappy feelings with happy ones, lying to ourselves that time will heal our hurt once we tuck it away and ignore that it exists. But the speaker was making the point that we need to lean into our feelings and name what they are. And that grief or any unhappy emotion is part of having healthy relationships. After one of Jesus's good friends, Lazarus dies, the gospel of John tells us he wept.

"When Jesus saw her weeping, and the Jews who had come along with her also weeping, he was deeply moved in spirit and troubled. "Where have you laid him?" he asked. "Come and see, Lord," they replied. Jesus wept."

Jesus grieved and leaned in to his emotions. We should too.

There's another reason why learning to feel and name our emotions matters. Because when we grow more emotionally aware it keeps others from having to experience the effect of our unexpressed grief. If we let things build up inside us, burying them away trying to "forget" about them, they will eventually explode. Not allowing ourselves to experience our emotions in a healthy way strains our relationships. The message from church ended with the speaker saying.

1. We must feel our feelings and express them freely.

2. We must slow down to review the root of our grief asking ourselves, "What did I actually lose?"

3. And then invite the Lord to heal our wounds of grief and losses.

Through this sermon I was reminded of the importance of not keeping things to myself, of feeling my feelings and not burying them away somewhere because eventually they will show back up again. The healthiest display and expression of emotions will lead to the healthiest relationships. Find someone you love and trust who is willing to be your listening ear as you process what you are feeling. And. invite

God into the processing of your emotions, your thought processes and your relationships. This is something I am still learning to do myself. Make the decision to no longer ignore what you are feeling. It's healthy for your relationship with yourself, with others and with God.

Day 17

I don't know how you're wired, but I am a planner. My mind works on an organized calendar that involves everything from what's happening in the next five minutes to what's happening in the next five years. For me, there's some comfort in knowing I have a sort of plan in place. For the most part, this isn't a bad thing. But sometimes it becomes too much of a control piece. I feel the need to be in charge of more than I should have to. In times of change this can become even more obvious, so when I transitioned into college it got really bad. You may feel the same pressure this year. Picking a college, picking a major, picking a summer job, preparing for life after college—it can all get to be a lot, and we're supposed to be enjoying this season of life and soaking it all up!

If you feel the need for a sense of control over the future, these verses that I came across recently may be as helpful for you as they have been for me.

James 4:13-17 says,

"Now listen, you who say, 'Today or tomorrow we will go to this or that city, spend a year there, carry on a business and make money.' Why, you do not even know what will happen tomorrow. What is your life? You are a mist that appears for a little while and then vanishes. Instead you ought to say, 'If it is the Lord's will, we will live and do this or that.' As it is, you boast in your arrogant schemes. All such boasting is evil. If anyone, then, knows the good they ought to do and doesn't do it, it is a sin for them."

I know that sounds a little harsh. But the idea behind these verses is to keep us aware of the moment we have right now. Because the time we have is short, time passes by quickly, so what are we doing to make the most of the time we have right now? And it's a reminder that we are not the ones in charge. As much as we think we are, as much as we like to control things, God is the one who knows.

That's the reality. We are not the planners of our lives. And as stressful as that can feel, it's also a relief. God is so much better than I could ever be at making the plans. We are not the authors of our stories, and that's okay. As hard as it can be to trust fully and completely in God's plan, I am learning this is the best way to live.

No matter what next year holds for you, remind yourself that God already knows. Allow that to reassure you and begin to pray that over your life whenever you feel tension and worry about what the future might hold.

GERALD FADAYOMI

Day 18

Life in high school is pretty structured. If you decide to go to college, there tends to be a lot less routine and more freedom and sometimes that lack of routine can make parts of your life that used to come easily, more of a challenge. I found this to be the case when it came to my faith. Growing my faith in college has been hard. The biggest challenge I faced as I transitioned into college was the change in my faith community. Not having a church I was immediately plugged into or a small group of people around was a challenge. It soon became obvious that all I had was my relationship with God. Even though I was meeting great, new, Jesus loving friends, finding community in Younglife and my sorority, trying different churches to see which felt most like home, making time each morning before class to spend time with God, my schedule started to fill up and life got really busy. My schedule became more stressful. My friend's lives got busy. Their schedules got more full, just like any other college student. My weekends became more full than I was used to and I didn't find myself consistently attending any of the churches I had been trying out. As finals week approached, and I could see the finish line for the semester, I started to spend less and less time with God. It wasn't long before I realized I had put Jesus on the back burner. For at least the last month or so of that semester my faith was no longer a priority. As I look back on my first semester, I know I was more stressed than I needed to be, insecure in my friendships and in how I saw myself, more short with people, more worried and more anxious. In hindsight I realize that when I didn't take the time to slow down and center myself in time with God and allowing His truth to direct me and ground me, every area of my life was affected. Sometimes we learn the hard way that we are not meant to live this life on our own, leaning on our own strength and fulfillment. We need the Lord. We need his wisdom. We need his Word. We need his hope, his grace and his mercy. I recently saw this quote someone had written from God's perspective to us that said, "I don't care how far you have run, come back to me." At the end of that semester it would have been really easy to be hard on myself for not making better choices with my time. But this quote reminded me of how God loves us unconditionally. He doesn't withhold grace and mercy. Nothing we do, big or small, keeps us away from him.

Romans 8:38-39 tells us that,

"Neither death nor life, neither angels nor demons, neither present nor the future, nor any powers, neither height nor depth, nor anything else in all creation, will be able to separate us from the love of God that is in Christ Jesus our Lord."

Maybe you need to hear that today. No amount of good behavior makes God love us more and no amount of bad behavior makes God love us less. My life felt out of sync when my faith wasn't a priority, but that wasn't God withholding himself from me. His love never changes. He has his arms wide open to you in your highs and your lows. No matter what may stand behind or ahead of you his love stays the same.

GERALD FADAYOMI

84

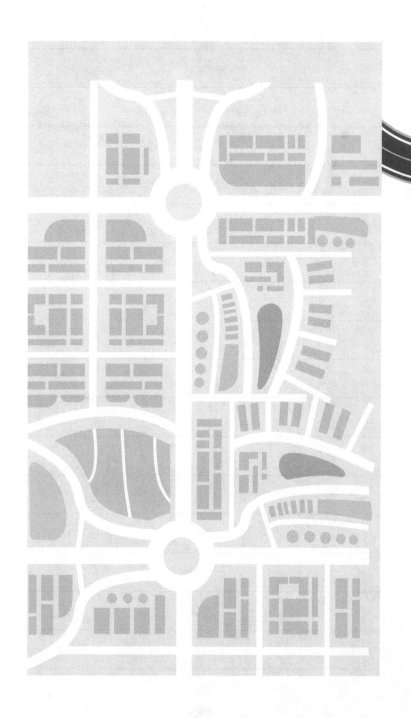

Day 19

I once heard someone say, expectations are our own worst enemies. It makes sense when you think about it. With every expectation comes the potential for disappointment. The more ideas we have in our head of how we think something should go, the more set up we are for a let down if it doesn't go the way we want. A better way to think about the future would to have an idea of what we might like, while still involving God in the process. Too often we write God out of our lives and our plans coming up with our own idea for what we want. But inviting God into the process is what makes faith so exciting. We can learn to be present where our feet are.

What would your life look like if you replaced expectations with appreciation? What if instead of setting yourself up for disappointment with expectations that may not be met, you set yourself up for grace, by thanking God for what you have and where you are? What if, instead of letting ourselves set and pre plan our future, leaving no room for God, we decide to be appreciative of the outcomes that unfold? I think we would find ourselves full of a lot more joy. I know this has been true for me. Over and over again I have tried to "plan" what exactly will happen, only to find myself hurt and disappointed when it doesn't work out. So I have started praying, "Lord, free me of any expectations I may have over this day. Allow me to be present where my feet are, not worrying or even thinking about the outcome of what's next." That doesn't mean planning is bad. It just means we don't put all of our confidence in what we want to happen because that's when we let expectations get the best of us. When we know our plans may not match the Lord's, but learn to appreciate the outcomes in our lives anyway, that's when we know we are growing. The Message version of Matthew 6:34 says,

"Give your entire attention to what God is doing right now, and don't get worked up about what may or may not happen tomorrow. God will help you deal with whatever hard things come up when the time comes."

For me, keeping this verse in mind helps me remember God is in charge of every outcome. And keeping expectations in their proper place frees me from the pain they can bring.

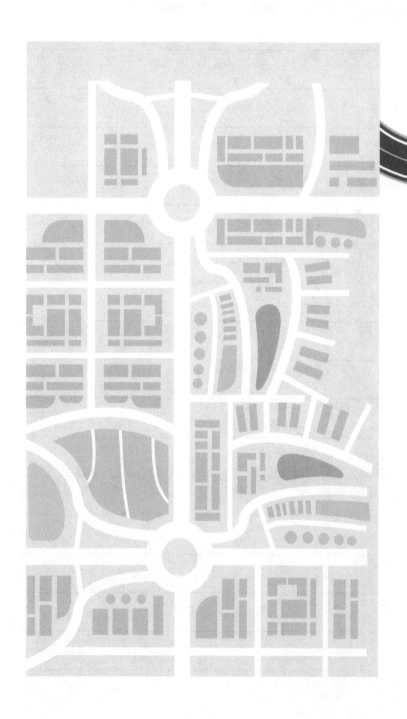

Day 20

Yesterday, we talked about managing expectations and moving from expecting a certain outcome in the future to being appreciative with what we have right now. This week I want to get more specific about what this might look like.

Maybe you have an idea of what next year looks like—the school you want to go to or the way you want your dorm room to look. Or it could be planning a specific conversation in your mind with someone, or planning a date with someone.

But the problem with expecting things to look a certain way, down to the specific details of a conversation or a relationship, is that we have no guarantee it will turn out the way we want. We make it a sure thing in our minds, but nothing has happened that should make us think it will actually turn out the way we want. So why do we do this to ourselves, setting ourselves up for disappointment and hurt when things don't go the way we expect?

I do this all of the time. I imagine things a certain way, and if it doesn't happen the way I think, then it feel less than perfect. It feels wrong or even bad. All because it didn't go the way I thought it should. And what makes expectations even more dangerous is when they aren't met, they can easily turn into doubts. We start to doubt areas of our life that may actually be fine, but don't feel fine because they aren't living up to what we expected. When we learn to keep our expectations in check we are more likely to understand that the Lord has much better plans for our lives than we could ever even imagine. When we are busy planning and expecting things out of our days, or complaining when things don't go how we expect, we are more likely to miss God's handprints on our lives. Learning to be present and enjoy each moment helps us to see where God is working, even if he is working in a way we don't expect.

Remember Matthew 6:34,

"Therefore do not worry about tomorrow, for tomorrow will worry about itself. Each day has enough trouble of its own."

Work hard to keep this in mind.

Day 21

You have probably already figured this out, but friends will come and friends will go. And as painful as it can be, it's okay. There are some friendships that will last a lifetime. Other friendships are put into your life for just a season. And even if it's hard, it's not a bad thing. Friendship, in all forms, is valuable. We can laugh with friends and cry with them. They can walk through the highs and lows with us. Some friends experience all the highs and the lows by our side. And some friends don't. Some are there for a time when we really need them and that's the purpose they serve in our lives. And you may never know the impact your friends have on your life until you are out of the season they were present in.

Maybe you've noticed this in high school already. That there are friendships that come and go. Some friends have been a huge part of really hard times, but when that time was over, the friendship was different. There were other friends that were around when things were great, but weren't when life got crazy. As friendships change, we need to learn to give each other grace. Either way, we need friends, because at the end of the day we have the potential to make each other better. In proverbs 27:17 Solomon says:

As iron sharpens iron, so a friend sharpens a friend.

Whether we're friends for a lifetime or friends for a season, value your friendships. Thank your friends. Love your friends. No matter what the friendship ends up becoming next year as things change, that doesn't make their role in your life now any less important.

Day 22

Some people really like new things. A new experience, a new place to live, a new school all sounds really exciting. But the truth is, there are things about new experiences that can be really difficult. One of the hardest parts about moving to college was the fact that I was completely stripped away from my friends and familiar community. And new friendships are hard. They're great too, but starting over with friendships is hard. You have probably spent the last four or more years in a place where you are a familiar face to others, and others are familiar faces to you. There is a level of comfort in knowing the people around you and them knowing you. And when you go to college you are starting from scratch. Nobody knows who you are or what you are like. It's a fresh start, but it's a lot of work too. So, while you are still here with your familiar relationships and friendships enjoy this last bit of time with them, the people who know you best. You will get a fresh, new, start soon that will come with it's own challenges, so for right now, take advantage of the fact that you are surrounded by familiar people. Jesus ended his last night, before being crucified on the cross, with his disciples talking about love and the sort of love they should have for each other. Let these words be an encouragement to you as you consider the old friendships you have and the new friendships to come.

"I've told you these things for a purpose: that my joy might be your joy, and your joy wholly mature. This is my command: Love one another the way I loved you. This is the very best way to love. Put your life on the line for your friends. You are my friends when you do the things I command you. I'm no longer calling you servants because servants don't understand what their master is thinking and planning. No, I've called you friends because I've let you in on everything I've heard from the Father." John 15:11-15

I don't know what the rest of this year holds for your friendships, and I don't know what the future holds, but I do know that Jesus has set a clear example of what it means to be a friend and we get to follow his lead. Not only that we know no matter how we feel we have a friend who loved us enough to die and rise again for us.

Day 23

Forgiveness is one of the hardest things you'll ever learn to do. But this time of change is just as a good a time as any to learn how to forgive. After this year, relationships and friendships are sure to change because of distance or stages of life or different interests. Because of that, it will be easy to hold grudges and get feelings hurt as things change. But instead of holding on to grudges or anger or frustration, make an effort to forgive. Do everything you can to head into this next stage after high school free of the burdens unforgiveness leaves us with. Whenever forgiveness feels impossible it can be helpful to remember what our faith is based on. As followers of Jesus, our faith is built on the story of the crucifixion and resurrection of our Savior. And we believe it was Jesus's death and coming back to life that demonstrated his power over sin and forgave us our own sin. It can be easy to think of forgiveness only in terms of us needing to forgive others for what they have done to us. And when we only focus on how we were wronged, forgiveness can feel like an impossible ask. But the story of Jesus reminds us that we have done plenty ourselves that we need forgiveness for. And if Jesus willingly forgave us of the ways we have messed up, then the same thing is asked of us, and God will equip us to follow through with it. In Colossians 3:13 Paul tells the church of Colossae to,

"Bear with each other and forgive one another if any of you has a grievance against someone. Forgive as the Lord forgave you. And over all these virtues put on love, which binds them all together in perfect unity."

The Message version of this verse reads, "So, chosen by God for this new life of love, dress in the wardrobe God picked out for you: compassion, kindness, humility, quiet strength, discipline. Be even-tempered, content with second place, quick to forgive an offense. Forgive as quickly and completely as the Master forgave you. And regardless of what else you put on, wear love. It's your basic, all-purpose garment. Never be without it."

The image of physically putting on these virtues is powerful. Deciding to forgive is a choice we have to make over and over again, day in and day out. And Paul even says we should work at trying to forgive others as quickly as God has forgiven us. As difficult as forgiveness can be, remembering we were forgiven first, and that every day we experience the benefit of having been forgiven by God, can motivate us to work towards forgiving others.

Day 24

In this busy season of balancing school, friends, family, faith and relationships at the end of your senior year, it can be really easy to fall into a life consumed by distraction. The worst part of distraction is how often we fall into it without even realizing it. Our minds start to drift somewhere. Without even thinking about it, we pick up our phones to start doing mindless scrolling. We over schedule our lives so there's no time to be still and focus on what really matters. Distraction can slowly seep into all areas of our lives. In school, family, the future, and friendships, our minds can be taken off of the important things and consumed by the less important things. To live a life where we weren't distracted would mean being more purposeful about fixing our eyes on Jesus. And with our eyes fixed on Jesus we will get back something distraction can take from us: perspective. Learning to see everything around us through a focus on Jesus allows us to see what is a distraction from what matters and what isn't. We can make better decisions over what to do with our time and attention. So what would surrendering your academic life completely to Jesus look like? It would probably eliminate a lot of stress and worry. What would surrendering your social life look like? It would probably result in a lot less self doubt and comparison. What would surrendering your home life completely to Jesus look like? It would probably strengthen your relationships with your family, or at least allow you to show more grace to one another and work harder for peace between you and everyone in your family. What would surrendering your dating life look like? It would probably help you desire the right things and the right people and help you draw healthy boundaries in the relationships you are in. The Message version of Matthew 16:24-27 says,

> "Then Jesus went to work on his disciples. 'Anyone who intends to come with me has to let me lead. You're not in the driver's seat; I am. Don't run from suffering; embrace it. Follow me and I'll show you how. Self-help is no help at all. Self-sacrifice is the way, my way, to

finding yourself, your true self. What kind of deal is it to get everything you want but lose yourself? What could you ever trade your soul for? Don't be in such a hurry to go into business for yourself. Before you know it the Son of Man will arrive with all the splendor of his Father, accompanied by an army of angels. You'll get everything you have coming to you, a personal gift."

In other words, we can trust Jesus to know what is best for us. And to live a life fully surrendered to him, and not just in bits and pieces, is the best way to live.

Day 25

Movies—and real life—are full of mean girls who belittle and degrade the other high school girls or guys who are constantly tearing down other guys. Treating each other this way has become so normalized to us. But at the same time, we still feel the need for validation and worth from our peers—the same people who tear us down. For some people this is a bigger struggle than it is for others. But all of us, at some point or another, have found ourselves placing our worth in the wrong hands. Then, when those people turn on us, or those relationships are strained, we feel like our entire self worth is compromised. That's why I love what Paul said in Galatians 1:10

"Am I now trying to win the approval of human beings, or of God? Or am I trying to please people? If I were still trying to please people, I would not be a servant of Christ."

It's so important that we live for God's approval not the approval of man. We have to constantly remind ourselves of who GOD says we are.

You are cherished.

You are righteous.

You are beloved.

You are redeemed.

You are bold.

You are worthy.

You are a citizen of Heaven.

You are chosen.

This isn't always easy to believe about yourself. But what God says about you is true and does not change. When the world makes you feel small, remember the Lord set a place at His table just for you. When you feel burdened thinking you're not good enough, remember to run to the One who is your fiercest encourager. The Lord will fill your cup and remind you of who you are when the world around you makes you forget. And when He tells you who you are, believe it!! Let God's view of you be the one that sticks.

Day 26

Words are powerful things. So learn to be careful with them. Your words can build others up just as quickly as they can tear someone down. And when we speak words that tear others down, even if we regret it later, or apologize after the fact, it's impossible to take the words back, or undo the damage that's been done. Think about it like a tube of toothpaste. When you squeeze too much of it out at once, there's no possible way of putting it back in—unless you're looking to make an even bigger mess than you had before. It's the same way with our words. Once they're out, they're out. James 1:19-22 says,

"My dear brothers and sisters, take note of this: Everyone should be quick to listen, slow to speak and

slow to become angry, because human anger does not produce the righteousness that God desires. Therefore, get rid of all moral filth and the evil that is so prevalent and humbly accept the word planted in you, which can save you."

It sounds like an easy idea: be quick to listen and slow to speak. But it's much easier said than done. It takes intentionality and practice to listen before we speak, and to measure our words before we say them out loud. Our words are so powerful. They can be as sharp as a sword and as healing as a band aid. Proverbs 12:18 talks about this idea saying, "The words of the reckless pierce like swords, but the tongue of the wise brings healing." Think about the kind of impact we could have if we started to see our words as having the power to heal and not just hurt. If being quicker to listen and slower to speak means we are more likely to have a positive impact on the people around us, than this is a habit worth developing. Be slow to speak and let your words bring healing to others. Your words are precious and so much more powerful than you may think.

Day 27

Have you ever dealt with something that is out of your control? That can be one of the most frustrating feelings in the world. You want to fix the situation, or get people to see it from your side. You want them to just relax or give you a little space. You want them to act a certain way or understand you better, but you can't get them to do it. You can't get the situation to work out, and things just wont go your way. We all want to control things to a degree, and it's because we trust ourselves. We know how we would respond or how we wouldn't handle it, and we wish others would just see it or do it our way. Not being in control is hard, but it's a reality. The good news is we have a God that is in control of the out of control. He has more knowledge than we could ever have and knows exactly how to make things, even bad things, work out for good.

You are all around me on every side; you protect me with your power. Your knowledge of me is too deep; it is beyond my understanding. – Psalm 139:5,6

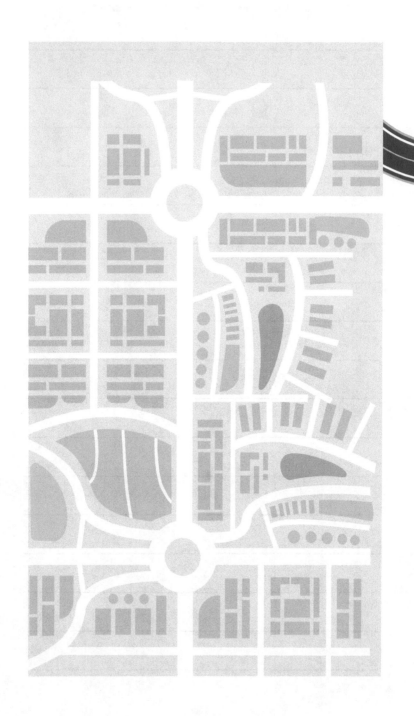

Day 28

A friend of mine always says to me "When in a fix, Philippians 4:6." I always thought it was a bit cheesy, but I've never forgot it. I'd say our world is in a bit of a fix right now. As I think about the season you are in and the season ahead I just keep coming back to the promise of Philippians 4:6,7.

"Do not be anxious about anything, but in every situation, by prayer and petition, with thanksgiving, present your requests to God. And the peace of God, which transcends all understanding, will guard your hearts and your minds in Christ Jesus."

Paul says that in every situation we can present our requests, our needs, our fears, our hopes to God, and in releasing those to God in return God gives us peace. I don't know about you, but in these days I am tempted to hold on to my fears, to try and figure out how to provide for my families needs on my own, and the more I do the more anxious I become. On the other hand, something happens when I release those things to God. When I can humble myself enough to say you're God and I'm not. You are in control and I trust you. When I present my request to God He gives me more of his presence and more of his peace. That reality is true for all of us today. Whatever requests, needs, fears or hopes you have present them to your Heavenly Father today and allow him to give you a peace that passes all understanding. I pray that his peace will guide you in these days and in the days to come.

Made in United States
Troutdale, OR
04/12/2024